# WONDER
## STARTERS

# Telephones

Pictures by CHRISTINE SHARR

**Published by WONDER BOOKS**
A Division of Grosset & Dunlap, Inc.
A NATIONAL GENERAL COMPANY
51 Madison Avenue        New York, N.Y. 10010

## About Wonder Starters

Wonder Starters are vocabulary controlled information books for young children. More than ninety per cent of the words in the text will be in the reading vocabulary of the vast majority of young readers. Word and sentence length have also been carefully controlled.

Key new words associated with the topic of each book are repeated with picture explanations in the Starters dictionary at the end. The dictionary can also be used as an index for teaching children to look things up.

Teachers and experts have been consulted on the content and accuracy of the books.

Published in the United States by Wonder Books, a Division of Grosset & Dunlap, Inc., a National General Company.

ISBN: 0-448-09656-0 (Trade Edition)
ISBN: 0-448-06376-X (Library Edition)

I like to telephone.
I want to telephone Sam.
I dial his number.

Sam's telephone rings.
I hear a noise in my telephone.
The noise tells me Sam's
telephone is ringing.

2

Sam lifts his telephone.
I speak to him.
He can hear my voice.

3

A wire from my telephone
goes to the exchange.
Wires go from every telephone
to the exchange.

Every telephone has a number.
I dial a telephone number.
This tells the exchange
which telephone I want.

Most telephone wires
go under the ground.
Lots of wires make one
big cable.

6

Some big cables go under the sea.
Ships put the cables there.

A long time ago there were no telephones.
Men had to carry letters.
They often rode fast horses.

8

Then men built tall machines on hills.
They made signals with machines.
The men in the next town saw the signals.

9

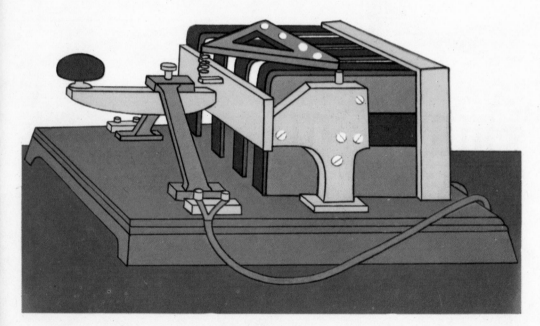

This old machine was called a telegraph.
It sent signals
along a wire.
You could not talk into it.

A man pushed a handle on the machine.
This made signals go along the wire.

One of the first telephones
looked like this.
A man called Bell made it.

Here are some more
telephones from long ago.
Your grandfather might have used one.

Here is a new kind of telephone.
It only has one part.

This telephone is like
a television.
You can see your friend
when you talk to him.

Some people use many telephones.
This man has four telephones.

This man has a special telephone.
Lots of people can hear him.

Trains sometimes have telephones.
People can make calls when
they are on the train.

18

There are telephones in mines.
The miners can telephone
to the man on the ground.

Most elevators have telephones.
You can telephone for help
if you get stuck.
20

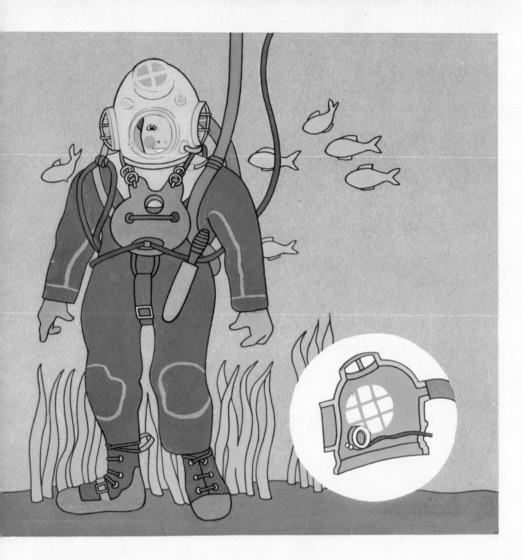

Divers have special telephones
in their helmets.
They can talk to the men
in the boat.

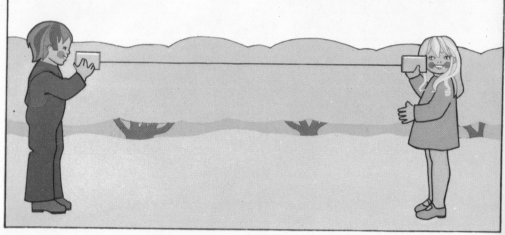

<u>See for yourself</u>.
Make your own telephone.
Use two tin cans and some string.
Keep the string tight.

22

# Starter's **Telephone** words

telephone
(page 1)

cable
(page 6)

dial
(page 1)

ground
(page 6)
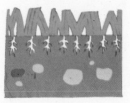

wire
(page 4)

sea
(page 7)

exchange
(page 4)

ship
(page 7)

23

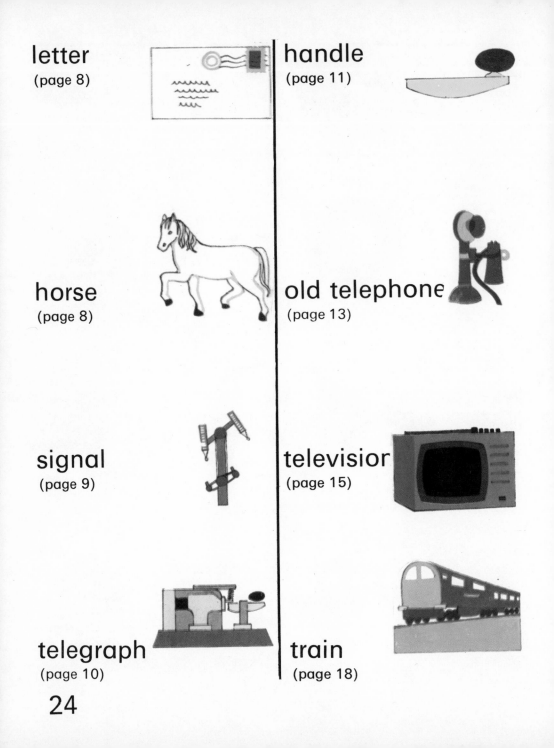

letter
(page 8)

handle
(page 11)

horse
(page 8)

old telephone
(page 13)

signal
(page 9)

television
(page 15)

telegraph
(page 10)

train
(page 18)

# mine
(page 19)

# boat
(page 21)

# miner
(page 19)

# helmet
(page 21)

# elevator
(page 20)

# tin can
(page 22)

# diver
(page 21)

# string
(page 22)